SAHARA

101 Facts About

TERRARIUM PETS

101 Facts About **PETS**
101 Facts About

Please visit our web site at: www.garethstevens.com
For a free color catalog describing Gareth Stevens Publishing's list of high-quality
books and multimedia programs, call 1-800-542-2595 (USA) or 1-800-461-9120
(Canada). Gareth Stevens Publishing's Fax: (414) 332-3567.

Library of Congress Cataloging-in-Publication Data

Barnes, Julia.
    101 facts about terrarium pets / Julia Barnes. — North American ed.
      p. cm. — (101 facts about pets)
    Includes bibliographical references and index.
    Summary: Provides information about different kinds of pets that can live in a terrarium,
including turtles, snakes, and lizards, how to care for them, and how to understand their behavior.
    ISBN 0-8368-3021-0 (lib. bdg.)
    1. Reptiles as pets—Miscellanea—Juvenile literature. 2. Amphibians as pets—Miscellanea—Juvenile
literature. 3. Invertebrates as pets—Miscellanea—Juvenile literature. [1. Reptiles—Miscellanea.
2. Amphibians—Miscellanea. 3. Invertebrates—Miscellanea. 4. Reptiles as pets. 5. Amphibians as pets.
6. Invertebrates as pets.] I. Title: One hundred one facts about terrarium pets. II. Title. III. Series.
SF416.2.B35   2002
639.3'9—dc21
                                         2001049495

This North American edition first published in 2002 by
Gareth Stevens Publishing
A World Almanac Education Group Company
330 West Olive Street, Suite 100
Milwaukee, WI 53212 USA

This U.S. edition © 2002 by Gareth Stevens, Inc. Original edition © 2001 by Ringpress Books
Limited. First published by Ringpress Books Limited, P.O. Box 8, Lydney, Gloucestershire,
GL15 4YN, United Kingdom. Additional end matter © 2002 by Gareth Stevens, Inc.

Ringpress Series Editor: Claire Horton-Bussey
Ringpress Designer: Sara Howell
Gareth Stevens Editor: Jim Mezzanotte and Mary Dykstra

Printed in Hong Kong through Printworks Int. Ltd

1 2 3 4 5 6 7 8 9 06 05 04 03 02

101 FACTS ABOUT

TERRARIUM PETS

Julia Barnes

Gareth Stevens Publishing
A WORLD ALMANAC EDUCATION GROUP COMPANY

1 Would you like to own an unusual pet? If so, you will have to be prepared. Terrarium pets need homes called terrariums, and they also need a lot of special attention. You will have to be very careful with them.

2 A terrarium is a large tank usually made of glass and plastic. A wire mesh lid and small holes in the tank let in fresh air.

3 You can create many kinds of homes in a terrarium. How you set up a terrarium depends on the animal that will live there.

4 No matter what kind of terrarium pet you choose, be sure to buy an animal that was raised by a **breeder**, instead of one that was captured in the wild.

5 The most common terrarium pets are **reptiles** and **amphibians**, but you might also like to keep a tarantula spider in your terrarium.

6 Snakes, lizards, and turtles are all reptiles. Frogs, toads, salamanders, and newts are amphibians.

Reptiles and amphibians come from different groups of animals, but together they are called herpetofauna, or "herps" for short.

7 All herps are **cold-blooded**, which means they cannot make their own body heat. In other ways, reptiles and amphibians are actually very different.

8 Like most other reptiles, the iguana (above) has thick, scaly skin to protect it. Reptiles grow a new skin and molt, or shed, the old one.

9 Most baby reptiles hatch from eggs. The babies look like tiny versions of the adults, and they can take care of themselves as soon as they are hatched.

10 Amphibians get their name from the Greek words for "two lives." Like other amphibians, the newt (below) will live both underwater and on land during its lifetime.

11 When it is young, an amphibian lives and breathes underwater. As an amphibian grows, however, it is able to breathe air and live on land.

6

12 An amphibian has delicate skin, which it keeps moist by living in a damp area.

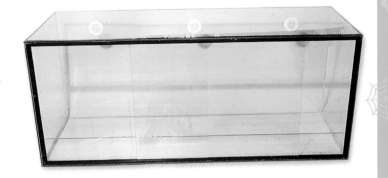

13 Your terrarium pet will stay healthy if you make sure the inside of the terrarium is as close as possible to the animal's natural **habitat**.

14 In your terrarium, you can create a mini habitat by providing the proper temperature and moisture for your pet, as well as any other features the animal might need.

15 Although the kind of habitat you make will depend on the animal you choose, most terrarium habitats require the same basic setup.

16 When setting up your terrarium, first make sure that it will provide the proper temperature for your pet.

19 You should also put a **thermostat** inside your terrarium. It will control the temperature so your pet does not become too cold or too hot.

17 You should keep your pet warm by using a heat mat (above). Place this mat under the terrarium. The mat should cover at least a third of the terrarium's floor area.

20 The sun sends out **ultraviolet rays** that are vital to the health of many lizards and turtles. A special fluorescent light tube, which is available in pet stores, can provide ultraviolet rays inside your terrarium.

18 Reptiles will need a spotlight so they have a hot spot for **basking** — a reptile's version of sunbathing.

22 The substrate is the material that covers the bottom of a terrarium. A desert habitat needs a sand or gravel substrate.

23 You can use your imagination to create a desert landscape with rocks and plants. Make sure the plants belong in a desert habitat and do not have any sharp spines.

21 For some lizards, such as the Leopard Gecko (above), the hot and dry **desert** habitat is perfect. This habitat should have a temperature beneath the spotlight of 97° Fahrenheit (36°Celsius) during the day and about 68°F (20°C) at night.

24 Place a small saucer of water inside your desert terrarium to provide a little moisture.

25 For a very different kind of terrarium, you can create a **tropical forest** habitat. Some types of tree frogs (right), lizards, snakes, and tarantulas will do well in this habitat.

26 In a tropical forest terrarium, the area under the spotlight should be kept at 90°F (32°C) during the day and 75°F (24°C) at night. Other parts of the terrarium can be cooler.

27 The tropical forest habitat is hot, but it is also very damp.

28 To keep a tropical forest terrarium moist, you should add a layer of wood chips, some moss, and a small bowl of water, and spray the inside of the tank with a light mist of water at regular times.

29 In a tropical forest, many reptiles and amphibians spend time in trees, so your tropical forest habitat should have some branches that reach to the top of the terrarium.

30 A **semiaquatic** habitat (below), which is part land and part water, makes a good home for most turtles and newts, as well as some frogs and snakes. This habitat requires a special heater to control the temperature of the water.

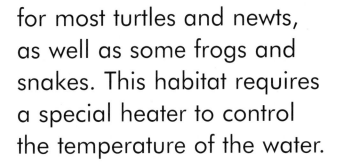

31 Turtles need a water temperature that ranges between 75°F (24°C) and 81°F (27°C), while amphibians prefer water that ranges between 51°F (10°C) and 75°F (24°C).

32 For a semiaquatic habitat, make a gentle slope out of rocks in your terrarium. Fill the low end of the slope with water.

33 You should cover the rocks in your semiaquatic terrarium with moss, so that your pet does not injure itself.

34 If you are going to keep a turtle in your semiaquatic terrarium, be sure to place a fluorescent light over the land area.

35 Some reptiles, such as the Corn Snake (above, right), need to live in a **savanna** habitat. If you create this kind of habitat, your terrarium will not be as dry as a desert terrarium or as damp as a tropical forest terrarium. A savanna habitat will also be cooler than the desert or tropical forest habitats.

36 The temperature inside a savanna terrarium should range from 75°F (24°C) to 86°F (30°C). You should spray the inside of the terrarium with water twice a week, so the habitat stays slightly damp.

37 A savanna habitat needs rocks, cork bark (below), and plants so that your pet has some shady places. Your pet might eat real plants, so be sure to use plastic plants (right). Coarse gravel is the best substrate material for a savanna habitat.

38 Before you buy your terrarium pet, you should learn as much as possible about the care the animal will require.

39 Amphibians and reptiles often carry **bacteria** called salmonella. To avoid getting sick, always wash your hands after you handle your pet or clean its tank, and keep the animal and its tank out of the kitchen.

make good pets. A Leopard Gecko, however, grows to a length of about 10 inches (25 centimeters), while a Green Iguana can grow as long as 7 feet (2.1 m) and needs a very large tank.

40 You should choose a terrarium pet that will not outgrow its tank. For example, a Burmese Python can grow to a length of 20 feet (6 meters) and is probably not a good choice!

41 A Leopard Gecko and a Green Iguana (above) are both lizards that make good pets.

42 When choosing a terrarium pet, you should also consider what kind of food the animal will need to eat.

43 Some lizards, such as iguanas, are **herbivores**, or plant-eaters. They should be fed green leafy vegetables and fruit.

44 Most lizards, such as the Bearded Dragon (bottom, right), as well as most frogs and toads, are **insectivores**, or insect-eaters. The most common kind of insect used to feed terrarium pets is the cricket. You should be able to buy crickets in a pet store that sells terrarium pets.

45 For small frogs and some salamanders, fruit flies are the best source of food. Most salamanders and newts will also enjoy a tasty meal of earthworms and slugs.

46 Because snakes are **carnivores**, or meat-eaters, pet snakes are usually fed a diet of mice or rats. A snake can swallow a mouse or rat in one gulp!

47 Most baby snakes are fed a diet of day-old mice or rats, which are often called "pinkies."

48 Today about 3,000 different species, or kinds, of lizards exist in the world. Only a few kinds of lizards, however, make good terrarium pets.

49 The Green Anole (below) is one of the most common pet lizards. Green Anoles are native to the southern United States and are sometimes known as American **chameleons**.

50 Although Green Anoles are not related to chameleons, like chameleons they can change colors. When a Green Anole feels threatened, its green skin turns dark brown.

51 A pet Green Anole should be kept in a tropical forest habitat. In the wild, the Green Anole lives in trees, and pet Green Anoles need branches to climb.

52 An average Green Anole is 9 inches (23 cm) long. Green Anoles need a diet of insects.

which means the lizard is active at night and sleeps during the day.

55 Unlike most gecko lizards, the Leopard Gecko does not have sticky toe pads on its feet. Instead, it has a catlike claw at the tip of each toe.

53 The Leopard Gecko (above and bottom right) makes a good terrarium pet for beginners. This lizard is easy to care for and can live up to 15 years or more.

54 Leopard Geckos are native to India and Pakistan. They do best in a desert habitat. Like Green Anoles, they eat insects. The Leopard Gecko is **nocturnal**,

56 A Bearded Dragon (below) is another good choice for a terrarium pet. This lizard is native to hot, dry regions of Australia and needs a desert habitat.

57 The Bearded Dragon has a "beard" of spines on its chin and throat, as well as spines running along the sides of its body. When the Bearded Dragon feels threatened, it fans out these spines to look fierce.

58 Bearded Dragons usually grow to about 20 inches (50 cm) in length. Although Bearded Dragons mostly eat a diet of insects, they also like to eat leafy green vegetables and fruit.

59 Skinks belong to one of the largest families in the lizard group, with more than 600 different species. In North America, 17 different types of skinks can be found.

60 Most skinks grow to about 12 inches (30 cm) in length, but some skinks grow larger. The Blue-tongued Skink (above) grows to about 20 inches (50 cm) in length. This skink is named for its blue tongue, which can be seen when it is hissing.

61 Most skinks do best in a tropical forest habitat, with a deep substrate of bark chips or soil covered with moss. Skinks usually eat a diet of earthworms.

62 Spiders also make good terrarium pets. The Pink-toed Tarantula and the Chilean Rose Tarantula will both do well in a tropical forest habitat.

substrate of soil and moss, as well as pieces of bark for hiding. This kind of tarantula also eats a diet of insects.

63 Pink-toed Tarantulas (above) are great climbers. If you keep one as a pet, make sure it has places to climb and build webs in your terrarium tank. The Pink-toed Tarantula eats a diet of insects.

64 The Chilean Rose Tarantula (right) likes to tunnel, so it needs a deep

65 The turtle family of reptiles contains over 200 different species. A turtle's shell covers most of its body, and the reptile will withdraw into this shell if it feels threatened.

66 Four different kinds of painted turtle live in the United States. Each kind of painted turtle has a brightly colored shell, with red and yellow splashes on an olive-green background.

67 Painted turtles like to spend time in shallow water and then climb on to rocks or logs. They need a semiaquatic terrarium habitat.

68 Although they eat snails and worms when young, painted turtles mostly eat plants when they get older. Painted turtles can live for up to 15 years.

69 The Eastern Box Turtle (below) is native to the eastern United States, where it spends most of its time on land. As a pet, it needs a savanna habitat with a shallow dish of water.

70 A Box Turtle's shell can close tightly in times of danger. The shell can remain closed for several hours before the turtle has to stretch out its head in order to breathe.

73 The Corn Snake (above) is a good terrarium pet for beginners.

71 The Box Turtle has an incredibly long life span. Some Box Turtles have been known to live for more than 100 years!

74 Corn Snakes adapt well to terrarium life. They like warmth and need a bowl of water for bathing.

72 Many people think snakes are the most exotic of terrarium pets. More than 2,000 species of snakes exist in the world.

75 The Garter Snake (right) has stripes running down its body. In the wild, this small snake usually lives near water.

76 Garter snakes need warmth and easy access to water. In the wild, garter snakes eat fish, which they catch with their sharp, curved teeth.

77 The Milk Snake (top, right) can grow up to 4 feet (1.2 m) in length. Milk Snakes can often be found living near barns that hold cattle.

78 People once thought Milk Snakes drank cow's milk. In fact, they feed on the mice and rats that live near cows in barns.

79 Snakes do not need to eat every day. For example, adult Corn Snakes and Milk Snakes only need to be fed every two weeks.

82 At first, frog and toad tadpoles live entirely underwater. Like fish, they have **gills** so they can breathe in water.

80 Frogs (above) and toads are members of the Anura family, a group of amphibians that do not have tails.

83 A tadpole becomes an adult frog or toad by going through a process called a **metamorphosis**. The gills disappear, newly formed lungs breathe air, and the front legs develop.

81 Frogs and toads lay their eggs in water. **Tadpoles** (right) hatch from these eggs. They are very different from adult frogs and toads.

84 At first, tadpoles eat tiny green plants called algae that grow in water. As tadpoles get older, they also eat small worms.

85 The metamorphosis of a tadpole into an adult frog or toad may take several weeks or longer to be completed.

86 The Green Tree Frog (right) is popular as a terrarium pet. The skin of a Green Tree Frog is normally light green in color, but the skin becomes darker when the temperature drops.

87 In the wild, Green Tree Frogs live in trees. Pet Green Tree Frogs need branches and plants for climbing.

88 In the wild, male Green Tree Frogs sometimes make loud, duck-like calls before a storm, so Green Tree Frogs are also known as "rain frogs."

89 Salamanders and and newts belong to the Caudata family of amphibians, and they have tails. Scientists often refer to newts as salamanders, but the two amphibians are slightly different.

90 The newt (above, right) spends most of its adult life in water. A salamander, on the other hand, leaves the water as soon as it is fully grown. Although salamanders live on land, they do return to the water to breed and lay their eggs.

91 Salamanders are often mistaken for lizards. Unlike the lizard, however, the salamander has smooth, moist skin and no claws. Salamanders can also live in much cooler places than lizards.

92 Most salamanders are more active at night than during the day. Salamanders, however, are never very active. During its entire lifetime in the wild, a salamander may not move more than a mile.

93 When attacked, a salamander can shed its tail. It grows a new tail through a process called regeneration. A salamander can also replace lost toes or limbs with new ones.

94 Many species of salamanders exist in the world. Fire Salamanders (left) and Tiger Salamanders (above) both adapt well to terrarium life and can easily be kept as pets.

27

95 Fire Salamanders need a terrarium setup that has lots of hiding places. Make sure that you also provide a bowl of water.

96 In spite of its name, a Tiger Salamander is not a fierce animal. It is less shy than most other salamanders and can often become quite tame.

97 Red-spotted Newts are found in the wild throughout the eastern half of the United States and are sold in pet stores as Green Newts or Common Newts.

98 In the wild, the European Common Newt (below) lives in damp areas on land and goes back to the water to breed. Females may lay as many as 300 eggs.

101 You have learned a lot about exotic terrarium pets — but there is so much more to discover! To keep learning about these fascinating animals, you can visit your local library, check out web sites on the Internet, or ask lots of questions at a local pet store.

99 The Fire-bellied Newt (above) gets its name from the fiery red coloring on the underside of its body.

100 Newts need a semiaquatic terrarium habitat, with an area of dry rocks where they can climb when they want to leave the water.

Glossary

amphibians: a group of cold-blooded animals that includes frogs, toads, newts, and salamanders.

bacteria: very tiny living things that can cause disease in both animals and humans.

basking: getting warm from sitting in a hot spot.

breeder: a person who raises and sells certain kinds of animals.

carnivores: meat-eating animals.

chameleons: lizards that can change skin color.

cold-blooded: needing outside heat to maintain body warmth.

desert: a very hot and dry region.

gills: the part of a fish or tadpole that takes oxygen out of water.

habitat: the place where a certain animal or plant lives.

herbivores: plant-eating animals.

insectivores: insect-eating animals.

metamorphosis: the process in which tadpoles become frogs or toads.

nocturnal: to be active at night and asleep during the day.

reptiles: a group of cold-blooded animals that includes turtles, lizards, and snakes.

savanna: a hot, dry region with grass and scattered trees.

semiaquatic: part land, part water.

tadpoles: young frogs or toads.

thermostat: a device that controls temperature in an area.

tropical forest: a hot, humid region that has a lot of plant life.

ultraviolet rays: a type of light that some animals need to stay healthy.

More Books to Read

Amphibians (Wonderful World of Animals series) Beatrice MacLeod (Gareth Stevens)

Reptiles (Wonderful World of Animals series) Beatrice MacLeod (Gareth Stevens)

Snakes, Salamanders, and Lizards (Young Naturalist Field Guides series) Diane L. Burns (Gareth Stevens)

Tarantulas and Scorpions Wayne Rankin (Chelsea House)

Web Sites

Caresheet for Tarantulas
www.ex.ac.uk/bugclub/tarant.html

Lizard Heaven
www.lizardheaven.com/ index1.htm

Pet Reptile Information
www.petreptiles.com

Swantje and Sven's Herps
www.newts.org/~swan/ourherps. html

To find additional web sites, use a reliable search engine, such as www.yahooligans.com, with one or more of the following keywords: **terrarium pets, tarantulas, snakes, turtles, geckos, salamanders**.

Index